Inspiring Adults

Literacy, language and numeracy in the
museums, libraries and archives sector

Garrick Fincham and Jane Ward

promoting adult learning

MUSEUMS LIBRARIES ARCHIVES
COUNCIL

Published by the National Institute of Adult Continuing Education (NIACE)
(England and Wales)
21 De Montfort Street, Leicester LE1 7GE
Company registration no: 2603322
Charity registration no: 1002775

First published 2006
© NIACE 2006

niace
promoting adult learning

NIACE has a broad remit to promote lifelong learning opportunities for adults.
NIACE works to develop increased participation in education and training,
particularly for those who do not have easy access because of barriers of
class, gender, age, race, language and culture, learning difficulties and
disabilities, or insufficient financial resources.

For a full catalogue of NIACE's publications, please visit
www.niace.org.uk/publications

Cataloguing in Publications Data

A CIP record for this title is available from the British Library

ISBN 10: 1 86201 241 5

ISBN 13: 978 1 86201 241 7

Cover design by Creative, Langbank
Designed and typeset by Creative, Langbank
Printed and bound in Great Britain by Latimer Trend

Contents

Acknowledgements

This publication was developed through a partnership between NIACE and the three Northern Museums Libraries and Archives Councils. Our particular thanks go to Heather Tipler, MLA North West; Jael Edwards, MLA Yorkshire; and Amelia Joicey, MLA North East, for their assistance, support and encouragement.

Chapter one

Opening doors

Museums, libraries and archives contain a wealth of enticing and interesting treasures and resources that can be used to attract new learners and to stimulate and support them to develop their literacy, language and numeracy skills. Many people in England and Wales have levels of literacy, language and numeracy skills that exclude them from countless aspects of modern society. Addressing this deep-seated issue is challenging and complex, requiring innovative and creative approaches.

Cultural institutions can work with learning providers to use their buildings, collections and resources to develop exciting approaches to learning to inspire learners and support them to succeed. The aim of this text is to draw together examples from the three main areas of work of the Museums, Libraries and Archives Council (MLA), to illustrate the benefits of developing literacy, language and numeracy awareness and provision, and demonstrate how professionals in the sector can work with partners in communities and *learning providers*. This book will be of interest to people working in museums, libraries and archives. It also illustrates the potential and benefits of working in partnership with the cultural sector for learning providers, community organisations and others concerned with literacy, language and numeracy.

Benefits

Learners

Access to:

- a wide variety of learning opportunities, that take personal interests and motivation into account;
- confidence boosting and empowering experiences;
- broadening of horizons, and the chance to take part in unique, once in a lifetime activities; and

chances to integrate learning into their lives in a holistic way, by visiting museums and libraries in between formal classes, boosting progress and success.

MLAs

Opportunities to:

bring new, non-traditional audiences into museums, libraries and archives;

access staff training and continued professional development;

forge new partnerships with learning and community sectors; and

develop new approaches to museum, library and archive learning and the chance to share best practice.

Learning providers

Opportunities to:

work with museums, libraries and archives to signpost learners to formal provision;

attract new learners by offering non-traditional learning opportunities;

add value to existing provision;

access learning resources from museums, libraries and archives;

use museums, libraries and archives as non-threatening, community-based venues to host classes;

forge new partnerships; and

develop new approaches to learning and the chance to share best practice.

Chapter two

What is literacy, language and numeracy?

Why focus on literacy, language and numeracy?

The Moser committee report, *A Fresh Start*, published in 1999, identified the large numbers of people in the populations of England and Wales who have low levels of literacy, language and numeracy skills and drew attention to the links between lower-level skills and social and economic disadvantage. While the figures are necessarily estimates and some of the evidence is controversial, there is no doubt that too many adults in England and Wales have underdeveloped literacy, language and numeracy skills.

This matters because literacy, language and numeracy are often factors in perpetuating inequalities and social exclusion. Possession of these skills affects people's opportunities in life, the choices available to them and their access to employment, as well as to the economic and power structures of society. This means, for instance, that many individuals with low levels of skills have low-paid jobs and cannot access promotion opportunities, are more likely to have poor health or live in poor housing, are less confident in helping their children at school, and are less likely to use libraries and visit museums and galleries or to participate in their communities and in democratic processes. At the same time, it is also important to recognise that many people considered to have underdeveloped skills manage perfectly well in their day-to-day lives, while others do not consider themselves at all disadvantaged as they live fulfilling lives and contribute to society in many and diverse ways.

Even so, offering a range of opportunities to enhance their literacy, language and numeracy skills is important for all these groups. Extending these skills can be empowering and transformative. It can equip people to:

- gain access to a wider range of opportunities and options in all areas of their lives;

- meet the challenges of our rapidly changing society brought about by technological advances and increasing globalisation;

Need to Read

Need to Read was an initiative to explore and share the different ways in which museums, libraries and archives could contribute to the *Skills for Life* strategy. The initiative was launched in 2002 and was funded for two years by the Department for Education and Skills (DfES) and the Department for Culture, Media and Sport (DCMS). It was delivered by three regional agencies of the Museums, Libraries and Archives Council (MLA) in the North East, North West and London.

The aim of the project in the North East and North West was to coordinate and develop existing and new approaches to tackling basic skills that responded to the priorities in these regions. In addition, the project aimed to help museum, library and archive staff to support learners, tutors and providers, and remove barriers to learning. The project raised capacity in the sector through awareness training events and the delivery of the NVQ Level 2 Certificate in Adult Learner Support. It also developed good practice; small-scale innovative projects and raised awareness outside the sector of the role museums, libraries and archives can play.

In the North West, the MLA worked in partnership with Manchester Basic Skills Consortium to launch the North West *Need to Read* project. Pilot projects were held at Manchester Central Library, the Imperial War Museum North and the Museum of Science and Industry in Manchester. *Need to Read* was extended into Greater Manchester, building working relationships between learning partnerships, basic skills providers and their local museums, libraries and archives, through staff training. A steering group in Salford developed a sector-specific, one-day 'awareness training' course, including resources, which has now been successfully used by other training providers in the region.

In London, an in-depth research project concentrated on the library sector, examining their current and potential role in supporting adults with basic skills needs. The research provided strong evidence that libraries are already providing important learning opportunities for adults, offering them real choices about their learning, successfully complementing existing basic skills provision, and actively supporting the government's *Skills for Life* agenda.

- combat social exclusion by challenging the barriers that exclude them;

- take action for social and economic change at personal, community, workplace or wider societal levels.

The *Skills for Life* strategy

The national *Skills for Life* strategy was launched in 2001. It aims to increase the numbers of adults accessing provision to develop their literacy, language and numeracy skills and to improve the amount, diversity and quality of this provision.

The strategy focuses on reading, writing, speaking, listening and numeracy skills. English for Speakers of Other Languages (ESOL) is designed to meet the needs of adults who are learning English as an additional language. Most adults have what is known as a 'spiky' skills profile. This means that some of their skills are more developed than others; for instance they might be extremely articulate but struggle to read complex written documents, or vice versa.

Information and communication technology (ICT) has recently been added to the *Skills for Life* portfolio since it has now become an essential skill, and new national standards and a common curriculum are currently being developed. However, ICT is not addressed in this publication as it is still an emerging area.

The strategy sets a series of challenging targets to engage more adults and increase the numbers gaining qualifications by 2007. The *priority groups* are those at most risk of social exclusion and include:

- unemployed people and benefit claimants;

- prisoners and those supervised in the community;

- public sector workers;

- low-skilled employed people; and

- at-risk groups, including homeless people, adults with learning disabilities, some black and minority ethnic groups, drug or alcohol misusers and mental health service users.

New standards of achievement for adult literacy and numeracy have been introduced. These are divided into:

- *Entry Level*, which is subdivided into three levels, for adults with the lowest levels of skills;

- *Level 1*, which is broadly equivalent to NVQ level 1 and GCSE grades D–G; and

- *Level 2*, which is broadly equivalent to NVQ level 2 and GCSE grades A*–C.

They are supported by new national curricula for adult literacy, adult numeracy, ESOL and adults with learning disabilities or difficulties.

A new professional development framework sets out three levels of qualification for staff undertaking different roles.

- *Level 2* is for workers who might advise adults, signpost them to learning provision, or support learners under supervision of a qualified tutor.

- *Level 3* is for specialists in other subjects and teaching assistants.

- *Level 4* is for literacy, language and numeracy subject specialists.

Who are the learners?

As in all successful adult learning, literacy, language and numeracy provision should place the learners at the centre of the process, and it is important to recognise from the outset that literacy, language and numeracy learners are individuals with very diverse backgrounds and purposes for learning. They might want to develop their skills because they were failed by their school. On the other hand they might want to enhance their existing skills to meet the challenges of the more complex demands of modern society. Their reasons for learning might relate to *personal development*, employment, supporting children and working for their community.

ESOL learners are very diverse and come from a range of backgrounds that encompass long-settled minority ethnic communities, refugees, asylum seekers and migrant workers. They might have high levels of education and graduate qualifications from their home country, or possess only basic literacy and numeracy skills.

In response, learning providers must strive to engage with adults in ways that make sense to their situations and contexts. This often means locating programmes in appropriate and accessible venues, often in the communities where people live. These sites include many informal learning settings such as

The Vital Link

Need to Read (see p.10) was closely tied to *The Vital Link*, an ongoing national initiative linking libraries and adult basic skills run by The Reading Agency in partnership with the National Literacy Trust and the National Reading Campaign. *The Vital Link* is funded by the Museums, Libraries and Archives Council as part of its implementation of the government's *Framework for the Future* strategy for public libraries. Endorsed by the Society of Chief Librarians, the programme is building and promoting libraries' capacity to support *Skills for Life* learners. Taking partnership with the basic skills sector as its starting-point, it is focusing particularly on the way in which reading for pleasure can inspire and sustain existing learners and engage potential new learners. *The Vital Link* has helped libraries to develop appropriate book collections for less confident adult readers, either by selecting material from existing stock or including titles written specially for emergent readers. Guidance for libraries on all aspects of their work with adult learners is provided through an online toolkit at www.vitallink.org.uk and *The Vital Link* is supporting libraries in their partnership with BBC Learning for its three-year RaW adult literacy campaign. It is also developing a range of partnership models between libraries, literacy, language and numeracy providers and other agencies able to reach potential learners.

libraries, as well as learning centres and colleges. The *Skills for Life* standards and quality frameworks aim to ensure that wherever adults access learning they experience high quality provision presented by staff with appropriate skills and qualifications.

What is literacy, language and numeracy provision?

The types of learning offered range from very informal activities designed to engage and enthuse people who might be trying learning for the first time since school, to more formal learning. Some programmes are first step learning; a reintroduction to learning that aims to assist learners to progress into further learning activity. Short courses build up learning in small steps whereas other courses are more substantial. Programmes for learners who do not want to take exams recognise their achievements without any formal accreditation, whereas others are designed to lead to a national qualification.

Literacy, language and numeracy can be offered as *discrete subjects* in their own right. A wide range of contexts, topics and issues related to the learners' interests can be used as a vehicle for the teaching; for example, material from

National Museums Liverpool, Skills for Life maths and English packs

National Museums Liverpool, working in partnership with tutors from Liverpool Community College, have developed resources for adults seeking to improve their literacy, language and numeracy skills. The resources were developed through the Celebrating Diversity project funded by the Paul Hamlyn Foundation.

The packs are based upon the collections of the Museum Liverpool of Life, HM Customs and Excise Museum and Merseyside Maritime Museum. The content is based around adult themes. For example the maths pack is themed around HM Customs and Excise museum, and features questions about calculating the odds on horse racing and roulette. The English pack is based on the collections of the Museum of Liverpool Life, and covers a range of subjects related to the history and culture of the city.

The materials are aimed at Entry Level 3 and Level 1, and are mapped to the new Adult Core Literacy and Numeracy curricula. The resources are designed to be flexible, and are appropriate for use in the museum and in community venues, as well as in Liverpool's networks of drop-in study centres. They have been designed to be both freely available and accessible, and have been specifically created as a photocopiable resource. They are also being placed on the National Museums Liverpool website as PDF files, from where they can be downloaded.

The museums involved have been particularly pleased with the ongoing partnership that has been forged with Liverpool Community College.

collections could be used as inspirations for reading, writing and/or speaking activities.

Another approach is to combine the development of literacy, language and numeracy skills with another learning programme. This is known as *embedded* literacy, language and/or numeracy. In this type of provision, the learners' aims and outcomes are related to both subject areas and the literacy, language and numeracy elements are explicit. An example of this might be a local history programme which aims to develop both research skills and the reading skills needed to access and fully understand a range of evidence and documents. You can find out more about these approaches in *Developing Embedded Literacy, Language and Numeracy: Supporting Achievement* (Eldred, 2005).

Museums, libraries and archives are well placed to offer imaginative learning opportunities and it is clear that staff in museums and libraries already support many learning activities. We hope that this book will provide some background information and ideas to assist them to engage more confidently and knowledgeably with the *Skills for Life* agenda. The 'Further reading and surfing' section on p. 73 points to sources where you can find more detailed and in-depth information.

© MLA, photographer Jonathan Goldberg

Chapter three

Learning in the MLA sector

The current situation in the MLA sector

"Learning is a process of active engagement with experience. It is what people do when they want to make sense of the world. It may involve the development or deepening of skills, knowledge, understanding, awareness, values, ideas and feelings, or an increase in the capacity to reflect. Effective learning leads to change, development and the desire to learn more.

(*Inspiring Learning for All*, at: www.inspiringlearningforall.gov.uk)

Museums, libraries and archives are unique and special resources that can be used to inspire and facilitate learning in its broadest sense. They can provide settings, resources and inspirations for a wide-reaching and diverse range of both *informal* and more *formal learning* activities. This means that they are especially well placed to contribute to learning activities that support adults to develop their literacy, language and numeracy skills, especially by working with providers to attract adults who are deterred by the prospect of formal institution-based learning, or people, especially some ESOL learners who are attracted to know more about history and cultures through cultural institutions.

The launch of the *Inspiring Learning for All* framework in 2004 reflected an increasing commitment to the importance of the learning role of museums, libraries and archives that has been developing since 1997.

In 2000, Resource, which has now become the MLA, published its manifesto, enshrining education and social inclusion as key aims of the cultural sector. Resource went on to publish *Using Museums, Archives and Libraries to Develop a Learning Community: A Strategic Plan for Action* in July 2001, a draft for consultation.

This plan underlined the fact that MLA institutions were about *learning* in its widest sense, embracing both the formal work done by educators, but also more informal educational work with communities. It encouraged educators in the MLA sector to think in a broad way about the impact of their work on the wider public, because museums, libraries and archives are 'safe' places to learn. As the draft report says, what museums, libraries and archives offer can draw people into 'social interaction and discussion … stimulate creativity, enjoyment, and learning' (p. 6). The report goes on to highlight the fact that museums, archives and libraries can be particularly effective at engaging with people at risk of social exclusion, many of whom are likely to have underdeveloped literacy, language and numeracy skills, and improving the quality of their lives. But there are also barriers that stop people using these facilities, ranging from money to people's own attitudes, as well as institutions' perspectives about their roles. Research that followed the publication of this strategy demonstrated that while the cultural sector can contribute to the social inclusion agenda, the approach has historically been piecemeal.

In 2000 this developing understanding of the role of cultural sector institutions in learning and education led to the decision to develop *Inspiring Learning for All,* which was launched in 2004. *Inspiring Learning for All* is a common learning and access framework for museums, archives and libraries, which aims to encourage the development of accessible and inclusive collections and services that provide learning, inspiration and enjoyment for everyone. The framework outlines a set of outcomes aimed at users and the institution.

Inspiring Learning For All – outcome of the framework

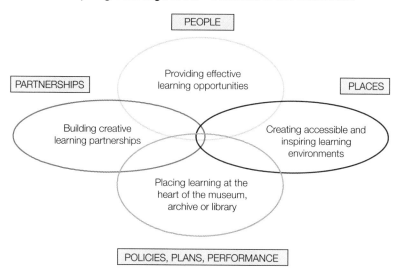

PEOPLE

PARTNERSHIPS

Providing effective learning opportunities

PLACES

Building creative learning partnerships

Creating accessible and inspiring learning environments

Placing learning at the heart of the museum, archive or library

POLICIES, PLANS, PERFORMANCE

The framework proposes a new way of capturing informal learning in a meaningful and consistent manner using generic learning outcomes (GLOs):

- increase in knowledge and understanding;

- increase in skills: intellectual, practical, professional;

- change in attitudes or values;

- evidence of enjoyment, inspiration and creativity; and

- evidence of activity, modification of behaviour, progression.

Learning activity related to literacy, language and numeracy skills fits well within this framework, which can help museums, libraries and archives staff in planning to implement *Inspiring Learning For All*. Evidence gathered under this framework may also assist learning providers to demonstrate the impact of their work. Current thinking can be summarised in the following ways:

- The cultural sector is a valuable social and educational resource.

- Because of their relative informality, institutions in the MLA sector are an ideal way of reaching those turned off by formal learning. They are about *learning* as much as education.

- Museums, libraries and archives are particularly well placed to engage with people at risk of *social exclusion*, and thus have a valuable contribution to make to more general goals on social inclusion and assisting deprived communities.

- Learning should be at the heart of what cultural institutions do, and to this end they should work in partnership with communities, learning providers and other organisations.

- There is already much good practice in learning.

Capturing and disseminating more evidence of what works will support innovation and the development of more consistent good practice across the sector. This publication identifies and illustrates good practice in relation to literacy, language and numeracy learning through museums, libraries and archives.

Chapter four

The MLA contribution to literacy, language and numeracy development

We will now consider the distinctive contribution that museums, libraries and archives can make to literacy, language and numeracy work. This will be outlined in relation to the *Inspiring Learning for All* framework in this chapter, then explored in more detail in later sections of the book.

It is important to weave literacy, language and numeracy work into wider learning developments so that staff can make connections between literacy, language and numeracy and other areas of their work. It is also important to take account of the national *Skills for Life* infrastructure.

Your role in literacy, language and numeracy development could include one or more of the following:

- providing learning opportunities;

- widening participation in learning;

- making collections, exhibitions and resources accessible;

- signposting visitors and staff to learning provision;

- providing staff training and development; and

- developing wider partnerships with providers and learners.

Inspiring Learning for All – the framework

MLA staff will probably already be working with the MLA's *Inspiring Learning for All* framework. If you are new to this field, taking some time to familiarise yourself with it should be very helpful.

The framework illustrated in the previous chapter is underpinned by the following outcomes.

PEOPLE – *Providing more effective learning opportunities*	PLACES – *Creating inspiring and accessible learning environments*
As a museum archive or library, you: 1.1 engage and consult with a broad range of people to develop learning opportunities. 1.2 provide opportunities for people to engage in learning. 1.3 broaden the range of learning opportunities to engage with new and diverse users. 1.4 stimulate discovery and research. 1.5 evaluate the outcomes of services, programmes and activities.	As a museum archive or library, you: 2.1 create environments that are conducive to learning. 2.2 develop your staff to provide support for learners. 2.3 promote the museum, archive or library as a centre for learning, inspiration and enjoyment.
PARTNERSHIPS – *Building creative learning partnerships*	**POLICIES, PLANS, PERFORMANCE** – *Placing learning at the heart of the MLA*
As a museum archive or library, you: 3.1 identify potential partners and the benefits of working in partnership to support learning. 3.2 work with suitable partners to plan and develop learning opportunities. 3.3 invite contributions from outside the organisation to broaden its appeal, bring new perspectives and extend learning opportunities.	As a museum archive or library, you: 4.1 identify and seek to influence local, regional and national initiatives relating to learning. 4.2 respond to local, regional and national initiatives in your plans and priorities. 4.3 demonstrate that your museum archive or library is a learning organisation through your staff development and evaluation processes.

Conservation on the Road, Liverpool Conservation Centre

Conservation on the Road was an outreach project run by the Conservation Centre, Liverpool and delivered to various community groups throughout Merseyside. It was part of Celebrating Diversity, a project funded for National Museums Liverpool by the Paul Hamlyn Foundation. The project was trialled in January 2002 during a week-long residential course for adults following the Adult Literacy Curriculum as part of a *Skills for Life* course. It was run in partnership with Liverpool Community College who gave advice upon how to design a session that would fit their syllabus.

A group of objects was gathered together and placed in a suitcase. The suitcase acted as a 'capsule' bringing the objects together to form a group of things that might have been found in a loft. Discussion of the objects began with a consideration of each one. This part of the session aimed to give people experience handling things, and what work would be needed in each case to conserve them.

The second element of the session was essentially detective work. The learners were encouraged to consider the objects as a group, to decide what they were, but also how they may have related to each other. Worksheets were provided to help structure this part of the workshop. The learners were asked to distinguish between what they knew about the objects (i.e. what was fact), and what was inference. Teaching the learners how to distinguish between fact and inference was a key aim of the session. Finally the learners were encouraged to create a 'fantasy' to draw together their facts and their inferences into a single story.

The project was evaluated via a report written by the project staff after the week-long residential, and through feedback from the hosts of the residential and the partner provider.

The following section illustrates some of the ways in which the framework can guide literacy, language and numeracy work. These developments should benefit local communities and individuals; at the same time they will also help you and your staff to develop and achieve your organisational aims.

MLA contribution to literacy, language and numeracy

People

Reaching a broader range of people

Museums, libraries and archives hold a great deal of material in their collections that is intrinsically interesting. Opening collections for the use of learners is a key way of contributing to literacy, language and numeracy, but also of encouraging people who may not be natural visitors to make use of the services that you offer. In the case studies at the end of this chapter, you can see how a museum, a library and an archive have 'packaged' what they hold to turn it into a useful *learning resource.*

One of the great strengths of the sector is that it can provide an informal learning environment and diverse, specialist resources to attract adults to take part in learning opportunities, often for the first time since leaving school. Many of the people currently excluded from MLA provision are from the same groups who are likely to want to develop their literacy, language and numeracy skills.

As you seek to engage with these groups, you will need to consider whether or not your organisation currently reaches out to welcome new and different individuals. It is important to think about how to make your organisation and the learning you offer both attractive and accessible to them.

But do remember to consult to find out what attracts people and what deters them. It is important that you don't assume either that all people from socially excluded groups have underdeveloped literacy, language and numeracy skills, or that even if they do they will necessarily want to focus on these when you reach them. People from disadvantaged backgrounds are just as entitled as anyone else to enjoy collections without a requirement to improve their skills while they do so. On the other hand, engaging with your collections can provide a safe and inspiring starting point to kindle an interest in developing literacy, language and numeracy skills or engaging in further learning. We will consider how to reach new people in the next chapter.

Learning opportunities

One of the most important and immediate contributions MLAs can make is to offer a range of diverse learning activities related to collections, exhibitions and other resources, many of which will be useful for literacy, language and numeracy tutors, because they are attractive to learners. These might include:

Key to Opportunity project, Middlesbrough Court and Central Library

The *Key to Opportunity* project was developed by Middlesbrough Libraries in partnership with Tees Valley Learning and Skills Council, NEMLAC, and NACRO, and Middlesbrough Adult Education Service to enable clients from the law court to use the library to access training.

The project was specifically aimed at engaging unemployed offenders contacting NACRO Court Help Desk in Middlesbrough Court about outstanding fines, although the project could also be accessed by any court user, or by referral from any another organisation or project. The clients initially attended their local library to meet with an advice worker, who could give them practical help and advice about the payment of their fines, and/or appearing at court. During this meeting they were asked whether or not they would be interested in undertaking any training offered by the project.

Middlesbrough branch libraries provided computer facilities, and Middlesbrough Adult Education Service made tutors available for one-to-one study with offenders wishing to learn new skills like ICT, and these assessments have led to the development and delivery of appropriate courses for project clients within the library, in partnership with the library staff. The project was also able to promote the library and its facilities offer.

David, for example, was 20 years old, unemployed, and lived in Middlesbrough. He had outstanding fines totalling £700. He contacted the help desk for help with his fines, and was asked if he'd like to undertake any training. He had done very little training in the past, and expressed an interest in learning how to use a computer and the Internet, so details of the *Key to Opportunity* project were given to him. He arranged to meet the project advice worker weekly at Middlesbrough Central Library and, while there, he joined the library and undertook computer skills training. David attended for an hour, for seven weeks, and at the end of it completed two certificated modules in Information Technology Skills. He said that he'd enjoyed the sessions because he didn't feel rushed. He felt a sense of achievement at completing the modules, which he had been able to do at his own pace.

- introductory visits, talks or tours;

- short, informal activities such as practical workshops based on some of the resources;

- learning programmes such as short courses;

- project work, for example working with a group to develop an exhibition or display;

- providing the venue for a class offered by another organisation; and

- volunteering opportunities such as helping to organise a display, guiding the public, or taking part in a specific project.

Literacy, language and numeracy development can either be the direct focus of these activities or embedded within them.

A key approach with all of the above is to work in partnership. Many activities will not be labelled learning, but don't underestimate the value of these experiences for giving adults a thirst for further learning. You will want to examine the content and format of any learning you offer to make sure that it is accessible to all people, whatever their literacy, language and numeracy skills.

Specialist staff from learning providers can assist you to do this. You can work in partnership to develop learning opportunities and new resources that have the specific aim of developing literacy, language and/or numeracy skills (we will cover this aspect in more detail later). Provision and materials that draw on your unique resources, your collections, galleries and buildings, to provide the foundation and context can add innovative and inspiring contributions to the literacy, language and numeracy field that inspire learners to discover new passions and interests, broaden their horizons and stretch their imaginations. They can stimulate them to develop new skills and to continue to appreciate museums, libraries and archives for themselves and with their families. You will find out more about using your resources to develop literacy, language and numeracy skills in chapter six.

Information, advice and guidance

Information, advice and guidance is a specialist service to assist learners to make informed choices about further learning. It is often known as a referral or IAG service, and any MLA institution can contribute very simply and naturally, particularly to the information element. Staff can be trained to signpost people to adult learning provision, including literacy, language and numeracy, and you can display publicity posters and information leaflets from local learning providers.

At the other end of the spectrum from signposting is specialised advice and guidance, delivered by specialist, qualified staff. Connexions is the service for young people, and adult guidance is provided by Nextstep. You could invite qualified advisers to provide one-off sessions or work with groups of learners in your venues. Libraries are ideally suited as a venue for IAG services because they already have a traditional reputation as a public information service, and because of the range of technological resources they now offer.

Places

Creating inspiring and accessible learning environments

Addressing the access issues specific to language, literacy and numeracy can help you to achieve the *Inspiring Learning for All* vision of accessible learning. As getting the access right means that people are more likely to take part in learning opportunities, this process can benefit many adults, not just those who decide to enhance their literacy, language and numeracy skills. People who feel comfortable and included are more likely to become regular users who are confident to make choices from the full range of services on offer.

To make this happen you will have to reflect on the whole environment and all the ways in which you relate to the public, not just what happens in designated learning activities or spaces, and you will need to ensure that your staff of all occupations and grades are aware of the issues and adjust their working practices.

It is vital to consider how to make your building welcoming and accessible. This means thinking about how all staff communicate with people and how to sign the building and collections so that people know what is there, how to access it and easily understand commentary and interpretations. Including content relevant to people, their cultures and communities in your collections and displays sends a clear signal that they are valued and welcome.

All learning activities should be designed to include people who might not be fluent readers or writers or who might speak English as another language, even though they might not tell you about these issues when they visit.

Staff need to know how to communicate with people who don't access written text easily or who speak English as another language. They should understand:

The Heritage Education Project, Clifton Park Museum, Rotherham

In March 2002 the Friends of Clifton Park Museum in Rotherham was funded by the Basic Skills Agency to run the *Heritage Education Project*, which aimed to encourage people to use the museum services for both learning and enjoyment, and get involved in local history at the same time. A major aim of the project was to establish a relationship with providers, and to help colleges to understand what museums could contribute to *Skills for Life*. Awareness training was delivered to both MLA and adult education staff to build the relationship between the two groups of professionals, and much time was also spent meeting learners to 'demystify' museums.

Partnerships were developed with college tutors, and adult education providers like Rotherham College of Arts and Technology, the WEA, Rother Valley College, Oaks Day Centre and Scope. Resources and ideas for activity sessions were produced through a collaborative effort between tutors, providers and the students themselves. The project also worked in partnership with library and archives services to deliver the wide range of workshops that evolved from the work. The project developed a range of resources for tutors, aiming to give them ideas around how to use the museum in their teaching. Different groups of lesson plans were created, each group of plans focusing upon a particular topic that the museum's collections could help to explore. The plans and supporting information were then put on a project website (www.focpm.co.uk).

Topics covered by the lesson plans were varied. Archaeology was one theme, with basic skills workshops run as part of longer courses, during which students also got the chance to work on an archaeological site, and contribute to an exhibition on archaeology with the aim of teaching writing and communication skills at Entry Level 3/Level 1. Oral history was another, interview techniques forming a key part of the project. Basic skills students were able to borrow MiniDisc recorders to record their own oral history interviews and so link strongly to the speaking and listening section of the Adult Literacy Curriculum. Transcribing the interviews afterwards gave students the opportunity to practice reading, note-taking and writing skills. In many cases, the students were able to create a booklet or small exhibition out of their work.

- techniques for effective oral communication;

- how to present written information in accessible formats;

  - write in plain English
  - illustrate with diagrams and pictures
  - translate into the main languages used in your community
  - design displays using accessible language and formats

- creative use of ICT; and

- other creative ways of presenting information such as pictures, videos, DVDs, computers, tapes and so on.

Partnerships

Building creative learning partnerships

Literacy, language and numeracy work is a specialist field and it is important to make sure that all provision sits within the national frameworks and meets quality standards. Working with partners is a good way of bringing expertise into your organisation as well as spreading your specialist knowledge and resources. Partners might include other organisations within the MLA domain, learning providers, advice agencies, statutory organisations or voluntary, community and faith organisations.

Partners can contribute in the following main areas:

- reaching new learners;

- resources;

- providing learning provision;

- information, advice and guidance; and

- training and staff development.

You can benefit partners. Your contribution might include:

- staff expertise;

- interesting and stimulating learning environments and resources to enrich the learning programme provided by other organisations;

- support to develop teaching and learning resources; and

- training and staff development.

Successful partnerships will be founded on mutual respect and appreciation of the different but complementary contributions each partner can bring to the work. You will find more about making partnerships work in chapter six.

Policies, plans, performance – placing learning at the heart of the museum, library or archive

It is crucial to equip staff and volunteers to connect with literacy, language and numeracy work, especially if it is a new area for your organisation. Staff development opportunities are explored in chapter eight.

New initiatives will add to your knowledge about supporting literacy, language and numeracy work though the cultural sector. Ensure that you evaluate your work, celebrate achievements and use the lessons learned to influence regional and national policy making and planning.

It is also important to keep up to date with regional and national agendas through the regional museum, library and archive council. They can help to broker relationships, develop good practice, advocate on your behalf and signpost relevant funding.

© MLA, photographer Jonathan Goldberg

Chapter five

Finding and working with new users

Introduction

One of the outcomes listed in the *Inspiring Learning for All* framework is to encourage a broader range of people to become users of your museum, library or archive than is currently the case. You might already have successful strategies for widening participation, but even inclusive organisations might find additional groups who are not yet accessing their services. Many of the adults who have no background of using, or even entering, your organisation are also likely to have underdeveloped literacy, language and numeracy skills. This chapter suggests ways in which you can start to include more of these excluded people.

You will need to consider how to reach out to people in the communities currently not accessing provision. This will involve developing an understanding of the many influences affecting participation and lack of participation. You will then be able to develop different ways of working in response. This might involve taking some risks and this should be factored into your development programme, but this kind of development work can also be very rewarding.

Who you are reaching – developing your relationship with existing users

One of the first steps is to identify who you are currently reaching – you need to profile your current users to know who you *are* reaching, before you can determine who is not yet there.

Determining who your users are is relatively simple; some of this information may already be available. Visitor statistics are often collected, including numbers of visitors and where they come from, as well as further information, for example about age and reasons for visit. You can also ask yourself and your colleagues to consider who usually uses your services, who makes enquiries, who are your volunteers? Some users might visit your institution for one reason, but be missing out on other services that you provide – so considering how you might broaden what you offer, or promote what you are already doing, might be a useful first approach. This should give you the beginnings of a profile of your users, and a greater understanding of the ways in which they use what is available.

Once you have identified who your users are and why they come, you can also identify who is missing. No matter what you are, or are not, doing at present, it is likely that you will need to give some thought to how to reach people in your local communities who do not currently feel that your institution is for them.

Who you aren't reaching – developing a relationship with potential users

Almost by definition, existing users will be at least reasonably comfortable with the environment in your institution, and they will have overcome any barriers that they encountered to accessing your services or collections. It is always worth asking such groups for feedback, because they may have had difficulties about which you were unaware, and which you can do something about for future users. They can also point to successful strategies for engaging different groups.

But having profiled *existing* users, you are in a position to try and work out which groups are not accessing your institution, and to take steps to try to understand why. This could take time and involve a good deal of work, and it may be that you will need to develop new styles of communication and new forms of provision in order to reach potential new users. In order to understand and overcome their exclusion from your provision, it will be necessary for you to learn more about what makes them feel comfortable. In the process, you may need to be prepared to experience some discomfort yourself.

You could start by asking yourself who from the following groups already accesses and who is not yet visiting your museum, library or archive:

- older adults;
- young adults;
- disabled people;
- women or men;
- people from socially disadvantaged neighbourhoods;

- people who are physically remote from your museum (for example, live in areas of your local community where they might find it difficult to make the journey to your site);

- members of diverse and newly-arrived cultural and/or black and minority ethnic communities;

- members of cultural and/or black and minority ethnic communities represented in the collections that you hold; and

- people of different faith groups.

This list is only a start. It isn't exhaustive, but it may help you begin to understand *who* you are already reaching and who is not yet engaged. You then need to think about *why*. The following questions provide a useful starting point.

- Are we reaching who we want or responding to who comes?

- How do we know?

- Why do people come?

- Why do we want them to come?

- What are we doing to encourage them to come?

- What aspects of our institution discourage them?

- Can we find ways of going out to communities as well as encouraging people to come in to us?

- How can we best consult?

Knowing about your local community is an important aspect of *Inspiring Learning for All*, and you need to try and be systematic about understanding your local area if you are going to be in a position to relate this knowledge to your profile of users. A good start is to contact your local authority or look on their website to build a picture of the groups you want to reach. You can also learn a lot by word of mouth – use the local knowledge of your staff and go to different areas and see for yourself.

Use creative approaches to consult people about their views of your service. You might be interested in developing their literacy, language and numeracy skills but focusing on a deficit is not a good place to start. You could employ local organisations and community activists to help with this work. Go to where people are: talk to them on the streets, visit groups such as parents or tenants groups, refugee support organisations, organise meetings or activities; take your resources out of your building into community spaces.

When you consult it is essential that you listen to what people have to say. Of course you might not be able to provide everything that people ask for, but it is important to go back and tell them what you have done and why. You might hear good things that encourage you to continue and extend your good practice, but at other times you might not like the messages. Even so, you must be prepared to take action in response, and this might mean changing the way you work.

View community links and consultation as an ongoing process. As your organisation becomes attractive to a more diverse range of people, think about training and employing learning or literacy, language or numeracy champions who have experienced what you have to offer, and understand how it could meet local people's interests and use their contacts and trust to encourage them to get involved.

Chapter six

The importance of partnership

Introduction

Working with others, or *partnership working,* is a vital aspect of the *Inspiring Learning for All* agenda, and will provide the key to developing successful literacy, language and numeracy work in museums, libraries and archives. Successful practice requires a complex range of skills, knowledge, resources and contacts that are unlikely to reside within any one organisation. For this reason, partnerships are mutually beneficial and a valuable way of working that allow each partner to share in what the other has to offer in order to offer provision they would find hard to provide on their own.

Creative partnerships, collaborative arrangements, networks, links and alliances with others can offer extremely effective routes to reaching new users and enhancing learning provision.

Partners and allies with local knowledge, connections and trust can help to reach new groups of people.

Partners with trained literacy, language and numeracy and/or guidance workers can bring their expertise, and sometimes additional resources and capacity, to your organisation.

Who should you work with?

Identifying partners is an important first step. Initially, try contacting your regional Museum, Library and Archive Council who should be able to offer advice on the organisations in your area that would make appropriate partners. You could also 'ask around'; use your own contacts and local knowledge to identify prospective allies and partners.

You might want to partner with other museums, libraries and archives to create clusters or cross-domain partnerships, to share expertise and pool resources for mutual advantage. The regional Museum, Library and Archive Council can also help to broker partnerships.

Partners who understand specific groups within the wider community better than you do can enable you to consult with and engage people from those groups. You may have specialist collections or resources that would be of particular interest to such groups. You could consider working with:

- learning providers;

- community groups;

- voluntary sector organisations;

- groups or individual community activists;

- faith groups; and

- health authorities/hospitals.

Your area is likely to have a number of learning providers who offer literacy, language and numeracy programmes in colleges and learning centres, community venues and workplaces. This can be confusing and make it difficult to choose your partner or partners. To help with this you will want to find out whether the organisation offers high quality provision, employs qualified and experienced staff, has the capacity to work with you and the flexibility to understand and work creatively within your sector and organisational culture. The list of possible partners might look like this:

- Local Authority adult education services;

- local further education or sixth form colleges;

- local adult guidance services, including Next Step;

- voluntary, community and faith sector organisations; and

- private training providers.

However, before you make contact with any prospective partner, there are a number of issues that you should think about. You need to consider whether you wish to establish a partnership with one other organisation or to bring together a group of partners with complementary contacts, knowledge, skills and resources.

What can you bring to the partnership?

Be clear about what you *bring* to any prospective partnership. This might include:

- access to your venue;

- access to your collections as an interesting and inspiring teaching resource;

- enthusiastic and expert staff who can support development of creative approaches to literacy, language and numeracy;

- staff time to develop teaching and learning materials based upon your collections;

- training for staff new to working with the cultural sector;

- a range of learning activities that might include one-off sessions and/or longer courses; and

- access for learners to other services that your institution might provide, for example guided tours of your collections.

What do you want from the partnership?

You also need to be clear about what you what *from* a prospective partnership. This will depend on what you want to achieve by working in partnership and what experience, capacity and resources you already have.

If you are talking to a group that represents a section of the community you have not yet reached, you might want to:

- use their networks to consult with the wider community;

- understand why that community has not accessed your institution, or the services that it offers, and to identify what actions you may be able to take to change the situation;

- spread the word about your work to the local community; and

- encourage demand for what you have to offer.

A literacy, language and numeracy provider should be able to offer:

- help with recruiting new groups;

- advice on how to open up your institution and collections to literacy, language and numeracy students generally;

- access to literacy, language and numeracy expertise on how to use your collections as learning resources;

- advice on how best to use your institution as a venue for delivering literacy, language and numeracy provision;

- opportunities to offer your collections/venue to students on courses run by your partner;

- access to qualified, specialist literacy, language and numeracy tutors to:

  - provide learning in your organisation

  - develop learning opportunities alongside your staff

  - help connect your learning provision to national standards

- access to information, advice and guidance services;

- staff training and development.

Working with partners: some good practice hints and tips

Once you have your partnership established, here are some key hints on how to work well with your chosen partner or partners.

- Ensure that the expectations, aims and objectives of the partnership are clear, understood and agreed by all.

- Agree clear communication and decision-making processes.

- Put in place transparent strategies for managing difference.

- Establish a proper timetable for the work.

- Make sure that it is clear who is responsible for which elements of the work. Make sure you know what information and evidence will be required for auditing purposes.

- Ensure that identified funding is allocated and make sure you know when and how you will receive your share.

- Do not overload the partnership – be careful to avoid calling too many meetings. Streamline any paperwork that may be involved to minimise the workload for yourself, as well as others.

- There may be times when you feel that you are giving, but not receiving. Remember that although you may feel you are not benefiting, you may be helping a group to achieve something that would be impossible without your support.

- Publicise the achievements of the partnership – this will show people that co-operation is working.

- Remember: to flourish, a partnership needs to be mutual. Both partners should always be able to say, simply and clearly, how they benefit from working with each other.

Evaluating your partnership

We will cover evaluation in detail in chapter nine, but for now remember that it is helpful to collect feedback from partners, on both the outcome of the work and how the partnership has worked. This will help you to develop your relationships with partners as well as to identify what you could do better next time.

Chapter seven

Planning and delivering learning

Developing literacy, language and numeracy skills though museums, libraries and archives can attract new learners, offer choice and provide a valuable complement to mainstream provision. The buildings offer interesting settings for informal learning, and treasures, collections and resources lend themselves to creative approaches to developing literacy, language and numeracy skills. This chapter will identify models of provision and teaching and learning approaches appropriate for your sector.

This is a specialist area and must be delivered by tutors who have appropriate skills, knowledge, training and qualifications. Most museums, libraries and archives will not be in a position to directly employ and support suitably qualified specialist staff, and should work with partners to develop their literacy, language and numeracy learning opportunities.

Models of provision

- *Embedded literacy, language and numeracy* learning, where the skills development is set within other learning programmes. This might arise from activities such as tours of collections, workshops or learning programmes related to your buildings, collections or exhibitions. The possibilities are only limited by your imagination. Some examples are:
  - interpreting collections and exhibitions;
  - art, drama or photography related to collections
  - music;
  - film;
  - creative writing;
  - family, local or cultural history;
  - reminiscence work;
  - object handling;
  - ICT; and
  - reading and/or discussion groups.

▦ *Discrete literacy, language or numeracy programmes*, where developing these skills is the primary aim. These programmes might use your collections, resources or exhibitions as the stimulus for the learning, and develop activities and learning materials to support this provision. These resources could be used in learning activities on your premises often offered by learning providers, especially in libraries, or taken out to other learning venues.

▦ *Family learning.* Here adults learn either separately or in shared intergenerational learning situations alongside the children they look after. Most museums, libraries and archives provide natural sites for the development of exciting and motivating family learning activities, not least because they are also known as places where families go together for leisure and pleasure. Many adults are motivated to develop their own skills

Tyne and Wear Literacy Resources Project

A partnership of five library authorities, Gateshead, Newcastle, North Tyneside and Sunderland, worked with the North East Museums, Libraries and Archives Council, Reading North and the Arts Council England North East to develop and deliver the *Tyne and Wear Literacy Resources Project.*

Groups of adults with literacy or language needs worked with library staff, professional writers and *Skills for Life* tutors to produce a set of reading resources for adults with low literacy levels. The resources therefore had the benefit of being created by people with an empathy for the issues that their intended audience face. It was also a valuable and creative learning experience for those involved.

Writers were selected because of their understanding towards the learners' requirements. Regular discussions were held with library staff, tutors and the writers to ensure that any emerging issues could be resolved quickly. The learners were recruited through existing literacy, language and numeracy providers and were invited to attend initial taster sessions. These sessions allowed the students to develop an understanding of what they would be doing in the project, and also reassured many of the tutors who were apprehensive about how the project activities would fit into their timetable.

The creative writing workshops led to the production of five different adult literacy books. They include poetry and prose influenced by art, local history and further by a desire to help their children, and taking part in family learning activity can be a springboard for developing literacy, language and numeracy skills. Local Learning and Skills Councils fund family literacy, language and numeracy programmes which could provide an excellent opportunity for MLAs to develop work in this field alongside partner providers.

- *Workplace learning*, where skills development opportunities are provided for staff, usually on work premises and often in work time. Trade union learning representatives are often key to encouraging worker engagement and brokering provision. Considerable benefits to both workers and employers have been well documented, and this could be an important area for museums, libraries and archives to develop for their own staff.

other sources that stimulated the learners to write. A regional book launch celebrated the achievement and the collection is now displayed and available within all the library authorities of the North East. This has widened the reading choices that libraries can offer to emergent readers.

The project was evaluated using the *Inspiring Learning for All* Generic Learning Outcomes. One suggestion advised that the tutors and library staff should themselves receive training in using creative writing, which is now being developed. The project is a pilot for Reading North, and the work undertaken will hopefully contribute to the development of further projects of this kind in the North East.

"I've learned to take words and look at them from all different angles; how words can generate others and generate new ideas."

"I feel more confident in myself. My reading and writing has improved. I have come on a lot, and feel I can go further."

"I feel proud of myself – that the work I have done is good enough to be published and put on display."

"The good side is having fun with your work and making people laugh with your poems because some of them are funny."

Staffing

Tutors will usually work for a partner learning provider rather than be employed directly by museums, libraries and archives. In addition to skills in teaching literacy, language and/or numeracy, they must be confident working with the source materials. Staff from each domain working together as a team can be a very effective way of bringing the different expertise together to provide stimulating, purposeful, high quality learning experiences. It is essential to ensure that staff are trained and qualified, and you will find information about this in the next chapter.

What's Your Story?

This project, run by Kirklees Community History Service, aimed to explore ways in which museum collections, buildings and archives could be used to provide embedded *Skills for Life* learning opportunities for adults. The project was focused upon the area around Dewsbury Museum, which is situated in the Dewsbury West ward, an area in which there are identified basic skills needs (particularly in the area of literacy). There was a particular focus upon using Community History Service collections to encourage learning about local history

and heritage in ways which could support local *Skills for Life* activity. The work was funded through YMLAC, a grant from the Dewsbury West Neighbourhood Learning Network, and money from the Community History Service.

Working in partnership with the Basic Skills and Outreach Teams from Dewsbury College, the Museums Service developed a six-week learning programme which used community history collections as a basis for learning activities and resources which were mapped to the Adult Basic Skills Core Curriculum for Literacy. This resulted in the development

Learners' interests

Whatever approach you adopt, the starting point must always be the learners. It is important to ground the learning in their lives and to reflect their interests and motivations, at the same time offering opportunities to try new activities in an informal and supported environment. Staff can consult learners before the programme starts and in the initial sessions. Remember to revisit these conversations, especially in longer programmes, since interests broaden as people discover new possibilities and challenges.

of a *What's Your Story? Literacy through History* curriculum framework, following the OCN curriculum framework used by the College.

The programme was promoted in areas identified as needing support under the LEA's 'Neighbourhood Learning in Deprived Communities' initiative. Two groups, one consisting of individuals from the Windy Bank Estate, Liversedge, and the other from adults attending a weekly Sure Start 'Parents' Time Out Group' (a social group providing parents with the chance to meet while their children are looked after in a crèche), were established. Each group worked through the *What's Your Story?* programme, therefore undertaking and achieving the literacy core curriculum standards to which the programme had been mapped, but perhaps more significantly their experiences seem to have altered the way that the participants thought about the museum and learning. One member said that they were "surprised that there are things that we can touch with gloves," while another was "surprised how much has survived." Others were wary at first, asking at the first meeting whether they would have to write essays, but by working through the programme they became genuinely interested in the history of their local area, rather than worried about learning. The delivery of the programme with the support of College basic skills staff also provided the opportunity for progression for learners.

Organisations involved locally with providing adults with learning provision and other neighbourhood regeneration services now see the museum as an important learning and community resource, and are interested in future partnerships, while other Neighbourhood Learning Initiative areas are looking at adopting the programme.

Initial assessment

It is important to find out what skills and knowledge learners want to acquire. Formal literacy, language and numeracy assessments should only be carried out by trained tutors (a role which will probably be performed by a partner organisation). Understanding what prospective students can or cannot do is important to designing relevant and stimulating learning experiences. The most positive place to start is to identify what prospective learners can do already. This might relate to their literacy, language and numeracy skills, but it is important to also recognise that they might have highly developed skills or knowledge related to collections and resources; knowing the history of an area perhaps, or a gift for creative skills such as art or photography. This enables tutors to discuss building skills from a sound base rather than starting from a deficit focus on what they can't do. These processes, which are known as screening and initial assessment, should use appropriate methods, for instance discussion with learners, and informal engagement activities, and do not have to involve formal testing methods.

Planning learning

Programmes can then be planned to reflect learners' aims and interests. Collections and resources are a very rich source of learning material, and can be used either to develop more understanding of their content or as a starting point to spin off in different directions, for instance as a stimulus for producing art works or creative writing.

Your learning offers could take many forms, including:

- short episodes of learning such as taster sessions or workshops;

- courses of different lengths;

- 'drop-in' learning activities where learners can attend at times to suit them rather than fixed sessions; and

- project-based provision where learners work together to create something such as a display, an exhibition, a collection of artefacts, a radio programme, newspaper or magazine.

Skills for Life Project, Manchester Central Libraries

The aim of the Manchester Central Libraries *Skills for Life* Project was to engage with learners with literacy skills needs, and to design a course which would allow the library to offer its collections as a learning and teaching resource. A two-session course was designed in collaboration with tutors from Action for Employment, who have students from a wide variety of backgrounds, and with different levels of literacy skills.

The course used the 'hook' of local history to interest the students, with a focus upon using the libraries computerised collection of photographs from different periods as a learning resource, with input from the libraries ICT team. Some students were even enrolled during the session for further computer training sessions. Each student was then encouraged to take an old image (from the 1950s, 60s or 70s) of an area of the city that interested them, and to write something about it. Single-use disposable cameras were also given out to take a photograph of how that area looked today. In a subsequent session writings inspired by the photographs were shared by the group. Alongside the development of the two-session course a number of training opportunities were provided for MLIS staff, offered by the Basic Skills Consortium.

In evaluating the project, the library service felt that it had established good links with providers, and hope that these links will develop into a partnership. Building on the work of the project, local history days are being run in partnership with Manchester Adult Education Service (MAES), and a regular local history class is now being run at a city library in partnership with the service. The library service now intends to develop a cohesive adult learning strategy to provide citywide services, and an individual is in post with a remit covering engagement with those with skills needs.

Learning outcomes

What the learners want to achieve are usually referred to as *learning outcomes*. You can negotiate both group and individual outcomes relating to:

▢ the subject content;

▢ personal development, for instance becoming more confident;

▢ literacy, language and/or numeracy skills.

The balance of these outcomes will vary depending on the level and type of programme, and literacy, language and numeracy outcomes will be more emphasised in a discrete programme than in an initial embedded activity. However, all activities can be related to the skills and levels set out in the national adult literacy, numeracy and ESOL core curricula. These curricula contain descriptors of the skills at different levels, but the context and content are not specified, allowing a great deal of flexibility and opportunity to devise creative programmes.

The literacy curriculum encompasses speaking and listening skills as well as reading and writing, and learning through your sector lends itself to developing all these skills. Learning in MLA buildings and using your resources provide ample opportunities for enhancing *speaking and listening* skills such as understanding and providing information, instructions and directions, describing objects, asking and answering questions and taking part in discussion and debate. *Reading and writing* skills can be developed through reading signs and many different types of documents, writing about collections, preparing exhibitions or displays. *Numeracy* skills can be enhanced through engagement with numerical content in information relating to buildings, commentary on exhibits and the content of archive documents, and object handling (for example, through measurement).

Teaching approaches

It is important to consult partners to select teaching and learning approaches most suitable for the learners you are working with.

▢ Group learning enables learners to develop a collaborative approach to learning in which they support each other and have opportunities to engage in discussion, debate and critical reflection with peers, share experiences, ideas and views and celebrate each other's progress. It is particularly important for supporting ESOL learners to develop speaking and listening skills.

▪ Individual elements to programmes and tuition enable the learners to work at their own pace and focus on their specific interests, aims and aspirations.

▪ Self-directed learning though ICT is a flexible means of providing learning for individuals who prefer this method of learning and/or whose circumstances mean they need to attend on a flexible, drop-in basis. However, many adults rely on tutor support to enable them to develop their skills.

▪ A blend of the above can be the most effective means of ensuring supportive learner-focused provision.

Teachers are crucial to successful learning. Some qualities they need are a commitment to consulting and listening to learners, well-developed interpersonal skills, creativity, enthusiasm, knowledge of their subject and confidence in using resources and materials.

Adults entering a new learning situation, often for the first time since leaving school, and perhaps with negative experiences of the formal education system, might understandably be feeling apprehensive. This can be intensified if the focus is on something they feel they do not do so well such as particular literacy or numeracy skills. However, not all adults will experience this. Some ESOL learners, for instance, might have experience of formal teaching styles and not immediately feel comfortable in informal learning situations.

The tutor therefore has a crucial role to play in ensuring that learners have a positive experience. Some strategies are:

▪ acknowledge and include learners' backgrounds, cultures and starting points;

▪ create a flexible, informal, relaxed and friendly atmosphere and make learning both purposeful and enjoyable;

▪ implement equal opportunities practices;

▪ devise interesting and inclusive learning activities;

▪ include interactive activities that encourage group rapport and foster collaborative working and peer support;

- provide individual attention where needed;

- know how and when to stretch and challenge learners;

- be non-judgemental and prepared to go over things more than once;

- build learners' confidence; and

- provide positive support and encouragement, and recognise and praise achievements.

Recognise achievements

It is motivating for learners to recognise how far they have travelled from their initial starting points, and it is essential to involve the learners in processes adopted to recognise and record achievement. Recognising and reflecting on progress during the programme is as important as final assessment because it encourages learners and helps them refine and revise their learning aims. Tutors should adopt creative, relevant and positive approaches, including:

- discussion and verbal feedback with tutors and peers;

- taped or video evidence;

- photographs;

- materials produced;

- exhibitions; and

- performances.

Two sources of support for staff working with learners to plan learning and recognise progress are guidance on planning and recording learners' achievements in literacy, language and numeracy (Planning Learning and Recording Achievement – PLRA) published by the Department for Education and Skills (DfES) and the framework for recognising and recording progress and achievement in non-accredited learning (RARPA) – see the 'Further reading and surfing' section (p.73).

Achievement should also be celebrated through celebration events, awards ceremonies, grand openings of exhibitions, public performances, or citations in magazines and publicity.

Museum of Science and Industry, Manchester

The Museum of Science and Industry in Manchester agreed to act as a pilot to explore an approach to delivering *Skills for Life* provision as part of an MLA initative. The museum committed to train designated staff to design a new course for adult learners with basic skill needs, to develop resources for the course, and to take part in an external evaluation exercise.

The staff training involved two days of awareness training, although one member of staff signed up to a full Level 2 certificate in Adult Learners Support. Practical training in delivering *Skills for Life* is also planned, as are short briefings for all museum staff on issues surrounding basic skills.

The course was designed by staff in consultation with the Basic Skills Consortium and a tutor from Manchester Adult Education Service (MAES), who delivered the course, and was aimed at learners with ESOL needs. It was delivered at a local primary school, but also included a trip to museum site, and introduced learners to local history and ICT, with specific focus on the cotton industry and industrialisation. Various teaching techniques were used, including looking at websites, worksheets, the use of vocabulary lists, a handling box of museum artefacts, and a tour of the relevant part of the museum.

The evaluation of the course was highly positive, and the museum plans to build upon what has been achieved by developing a new service for people with basic skills needs. It is intended to develop a series of sessions and short courses to be offered to tutors as a resource, continue staff development around basic skills issues and strengthen relationships with key partners.

Chapter eight

Skills for Life and the workforce

Introduction

This chapter considers the implications of literacy, language and numeracy developments for staff. A whole-organisation approach is the most effective way of ensuring that organisations are equipped for this role. This means that everyone in your organisation should understand issues relating to literacy, language and numeracy, know what contribution they can make and has training to support them to do this. This does *not* mean that MLAs need to be able to offer training around *Skills for Life* as this is best done in partnership with an experienced provider. However, raised awareness of *Skills for Life* among the staff of institutions covered by the MLA domains is important to embedding it in different aspects of the work. The success of this approach depends on:

- the active commitment and involvement of senior management;

- developing a strategic approach to embedding literacy, language and numeracy across organisation activity; and

- appropriate training for all staff of all levels and grades.

How can you achieve it?

Managers need to commit to integrating literacy, language and numeracy into relevant aspects of the organisation's work. This will work best if developed as an integral aspect of *Inspiring Learning for All* developments rather than as a separate area of work. Three keys to success are:

- Identify a champion from your management team and/or committee. They will keep the work live and encourage both management colleagues and members of the wider staff team to develop creative and dynamic approaches in this area of work right across the organisation.

- Appoint a person to develop a strategy. This will mean reviewing the different aspects of your organisation's work, planning to revise practice and introducing new activity.

- Introduce a programme of staff training to ensure that they understand the agenda and feel confident and committed to the contribution they can make.

Chapter four outlined the different roles museums, libraries and archives might have in literacy, language and numeracy work. Staff training will depend on the type and level of involvement. All staff will need some awareness training and some specialist input to enable them to carry out their roles. Sometimes staff from MLAs and the provider organisation will benefit by training together, for example in relation to developing context specific knowledge, provision and/or materials.

Teaching provision should be led by qualified tutors and be of appropriate quality. Your partners might employ the tutors or you might employ your own. This will depend on the amount and range of provision you offer, and your organisational capacity to support specialist staff. The national *Skills for Life* qualifications framework has been developed to ensure that the workforce and volunteers working in the field are qualified, and sets out the qualifications staff are expected to achieve in order to work in different roles.

Introductory awareness training

Introductory training helps to raise awareness generally within institutions about literacy, language and numeracy, and helps different staff to identify what they can do to respond.

You might be able to include basic awareness training in staff induction and customer care training, as many frontline staff and others who interact with visitors may well have contact with members of the public who find some literacy, language and/or numeracy tasks challenging.

You might expect awareness training to cover such issues as:

- literacy, language and numeracy and the national *Skills for Life* strategy;

- the importance of literacy, language and numeracy skills as a means towards active participation in society;

- cultural and language awareness raising;

- the relevance of literacy, language and numeracy issues in your work;

- literacy, language and numeracy within the local community, including the range of opportunities available;

- key roles and responsibilities in literacy, language and numeracy;

- methods of identifying literacy, language and numeracy needs;

- use of screening or assessment tools;

- how to signpost adults to appropriate provision; and

- how different staff can promote literacy, language and literacy through their work.

Introductory awareness training is widely available, and organisations providing this training should be able to customise programmes that reflect the unique context of the MLA sector. It can take as little as half a day for a brief unaccredited taster session, or up to 20 hours for the first Basic Skills Awareness unit of the specialist support qualification at Level Two, the Certificate for Adult Learner Support, which is nationally accredited. If you are planning awareness training with a provider, ensure that they can tailor the training to suit your organisation, for example by arranging a visit to gain an understanding of your workplace.

The awareness training might inspire some of your own staff to develop their own literacy, language or numeracy skills. Be aware that there might be some sensitivity around disclosure of this, or worries that it will disadvantage them at work in some way, and ensure that information, advice and guidance is available to ensure a seamless progression. In unionised workplaces, union learning representatives can take on the role of working with colleagues to identify learning interests and broker access to provision.

If your organisation or staff are new to working with adult learners they might also need development in some of the following areas:

- effective outreach and consultation strategies;

- communicating within the organisation;

- literacy, language and numeracy access issues and how to address them;

- how to support learners to identify their learning goals;

- how to use collections and resources for learning both on and off site;

- creative teaching and learning strategies;

- how to use ICT to enhance learning;

- learning strategies for working with adults with learning difficulties or disabilities;

- equality issues; and

- effective partnership working.

Provider staff training needs

Staff from other organisations will already have the training and skills to equip them for their teaching or advice roles. Training and development to equip them to work effectively with your domain will motivate and inspire them and help to ensure that working relationships are based on mutual understanding, and are creative and productive. It is important to find out what the training needs are as these will vary depending on prior experience of working with the MLA sector. They might include:

- general introduction to learning in the MLA sector;

- organisational induction;

- aims, priorities, and ways of working;

- resources and collections; and

- staff expertise.

Level 2 Certificate for Adult Learner Support

This qualification is directed at those who come into contact with literacy, language and numeracy learners in an informal support or signposting role and is the qualification that MLA recommend for staff working with adults. The first unit of the qualification has been designed to increase awareness of the *Skills for Life* agenda and the role of providing learner support, to provide the skills to screen for literacy, numeracy and language needs, and to signpost individuals to appropriate provision. Unit two introduces the participants to team working within the learning environment under the guidance of the specialist teacher. Finally, those candidates completing the full certificate will choose one of the three literacy, language and numeracy specialisms, and are introduced to the curricula documents and to strategies which teachers may use to explain or demonstrate literacy, language and numeracy skills. The choice of a specialism also begins to develop the candidate's own higher level personal skills as part of a progression route to higher level qualifications. In order to complete the full certificate, candidates will be required to demonstrate that their own personal literacy and numeracy skills are at least at Level 2.

Further teacher training

More in-depth teacher training is also available which can help to develop capacity to engage with literacy, language and numeracy. If your organisation is considering becoming a direct provider of literacy, language and numeracy, it will be necessary for relevant delivery staff to have appropriate specialist literacy, language and numeracy qualifications. It is more likely that you will be working with partners, and it is important to establish that their teachers have the appropriate skills, knowledge and qualifications.

- Qualifications are available at Levels 3 and 4 in literacy, language and numeracy. Each addresses knowledge and understanding of literacy, language or numeracy learning issues and contexts as well as personal skills. The Level 3 certificates for adult literacy, language and numeracy support are to enable staff who teach other subjects to support adult learners who want additional literacy, language and numeracy learning support. This qualification could support those employed in the sector, for instance ICT tutors working in libraries.

The Level 4 certificates for adult literacy, language and numeracy subject specialists are the full *Skills for Life* teaching qualifications required of all new entrants to the profession. This requirement applies to all those who lead learning in literacy, language and numeracy, regardless of job title or context.

These subject specifications only contain the personal literacy, language or numeracy skills required and the knowledge and understanding of the subject that literacy, language and numeracy teachers must have. They do not contain elements of pedagogy, i.e. *how to teach* literacy, language and numeracy. The practical teaching skills are interpreted through the same generic teaching standards as for all teachers, and those taking Level 4 will need to hold generic teaching qualifications as well.

Volunteers

Although this chapter is about 'staff', it should be noted that volunteers are an important component of the staff in many MLA institutions. They often perform similar roles to frontline staff and these bring them into frequent informal contact with potential literacy, language and numeracy learners. We will discuss volunteers in detail in the next chapter, but as far as possible literacy, language and numeracy awareness training should be included in their induction and training.

Chapter nine

Valuing volunteers

Introduction

Many institutions within the MLA domains rely on volunteers to support *core members of staff*. People volunteer for a range of reasons:

- enthusiasm for the institution and its aims;

- to engage in a social activity;

- to learn new skills; and

- to support others to appreciate and enjoy collections and resources.

Addressing literacy, language and numeracy issues in your work with volunteers could help make volunteering a more valuable experience for both you and your volunteers.

Volunteers as support

Volunteers can play a role in supporting literacy, language and numeracy work developments in museums, libraries and archives. However, they should, like paid staff, have access to appropriate training to equip them to carry out their roles, and you will need to identify the funding, time and resources to support this training. Developing awareness of literacy, language and numeracy issues can make your organisation more accessible and inclusive, and this can be included in volunteers' induction training.

People who want to volunteer for literacy, language and numeracy support should, like your staff, take part in Level 2 training. It is crucial to remember that people volunteer for a pleasurable experience; not everyone will want the added pressure of undertaking a formal, externally assessed training programme in pursuit of this pleasure. Make sure your volunteers understand what the training is about and the commitment you are asking them to make. Don't set them up to fail. They need to know the skills demands for successful completion of the course. If they choose not to do this make sure that other volunteering options are available.

Volunteers as learners

Volunteering can be a valuable learning experience. Volunteers learn both informally and through specific training about the people and collections they are working with and gain skills to interact in different roles with staff and users as well as carry out activities for the first time. All of these can contribute to gains in confidence and self-esteem. They might also become inspired and motivated to take up more formal learning opportunities.

Volunteering can also lead volunteers to new pursuits and passions which they might want to follow up in learning situations. As they volunteer they might find they want to hone specific skills such as ICT skills, or they might develop totally new interests through working with your resources and collections. Some volunteers also decide they want to improve their own literacy, language or numeracy skills, but don't impose this. Remember that people can carry out pleasurable activities without having to deal with things they might find difficult.

You can respond by:

- providing information, advice and guidance to signpost them to appropriate provision – if you don't have trained staff you might organise regular sessions with the local adult guidance workers;

- consulting volunteers about their learning interests;

- organising opportunities for volunteers;

- ensuring they have access to learning opportunities you organise for the public and your staff; and

- introducing on-the-job learning; for instance involvement in the production of learning materials for literacy, language and/or numeracy provision, perhaps based around collections that they are familiar with through their volunteering, under the supervision of a trained tutor, as part of a project.

Recruiting volunteers from literacy, language and numeracy courses

Your new focus on literacy, language and numeracy skills should result in more adults who are developing these skills visiting your organisation. They might be taking part in learning programmes, using your resources to support their learning or simply visiting to enjoy your collections. Why not offer them the opportunity to volunteer with you, especially if you are already geared up to work with volunteers? They could bring you a wealth of experience and local knowledge and contacts, and volunteering could build their skills, confidence and self-esteem or perhaps lead to work or training opportunities.

Remember to ask volunteers what they want, and not just assume they will want to be associated solely with literacy, language and numeracy provision. Possible roles might include:

- champion or ambassador for your organisation and/or learning provision who can spread the word in their local community;

- explainer of collections, especially when they relate to the volunteer's particular community or group;

- contributer to awareness-raising or training sessions;

- adviser on access – drawing on their own experience; and

- volunteer in learning provision.

All of these roles would enable them to continue to develop their literacy and language skills either in informal or more clearly identified ways related to the role.

Once again, it is important to ensure that your volunteers fully understand and are comfortable and confident with the nature and level of responsibility of their role. Volunteers who have recently been literacy, language and numeracy learners themselves may need customised support to make a successful transition from learner to volunteer, but this will be rewarded by an extremely valuable contribution.

Chapter ten

Evaluating your work: How do you know that it's making a difference?

Introduction

Evaluation is an important aspect of all learning provision and a key element of *Inspiring Learning for All*. Capturing the impact of your work enables you to know whether what you are doing is having the effect that you intended, what works well and what could be better.

Evaluation criteria

As discussed in our chapter on 'Getting started', it is vital that learning aims and outcomes are established for your work. What new learning do learners expect to gain from the experiences you have provided? What do you and partners expect to achieve? These are the criteria against which you should assess your work. Have you and the learners achieved your aims? Have there been any unanticipated outcomes? The answers to these questions must be based on evidence. This evidence can take a variety of forms, and creative approaches can be used to collect it, but before you start you must be clear about the purpose of gathering this evidence. It is crucial to show the impact on people; the experiences and benefits for the learners involved. You might also want to consider the impact on your organisation, staff and volunteers. You should try to find out what has been achieved, how people have benefited, what has been particularly effective and ways in which it could be improved if you are to offer the activity again.

What counts as evidence?

Evidence can be gathered by staff, volunteers, learners or external evaluators. It can take different forms and these should be appropriate. Questions to ask are: What do I need to know? What information do we have already and what do we need to collect? Who do we need to collect it from? Do we want collective or individual information? Will language or literacy be a barrier? How long will it take? There are many methods, including the following:

- A product such as an exhibition, display, publication or web page produced by students can provide a major piece of evidence.

- Visual evidence such as photographs can record the learning process as well as the final product.

- Different methods to collect views include:

  - web-based discussions or questionnaires;

  - simple feedback forms or questionnaires which will provide a concrete indication of how satisfied people are with the work, how they have benefited and generate ideas on how to develop the project;

  - informal discussions;

  - focus groups;

  - distributing sticky notes and encouraging participants to write on them what they felt about the project and stick them on the wall; and

  - producing group posters using words and/or drawings to represent views.

Generic Learning Outcomes

Generic Learning Outcomes (GLOs) are a key tool for gathering evidence of achievement under the *Inspiring Learning for All* framework. They were specifically designed to create a comprehensive framework within which to evaluate the impact of provision upon learners. Developed by MLA in conjunction with Leicester University (as part of the Learning Impact Research project), they fall into five main themes, each of which covers a different learner-focused outcome of provision:

- Increase in knowledge and understanding

- Increase in skills: intellectual, practical, professional

- Change in attitudes or values

- Evidence of enjoyment, inspiration and creativity

- Evidence of activity, modification of behaviour, progression

Literacy, language and numeracy work will contribute towards your achievements under the GLOs, and the GLOs can help you to assess the impact of literacy, language and numeracy alongside your other provision.

It is important to note that the GLOs are not directly linked to the *Skills for Life* and adult learning quality frameworks. These frameworks require evidence of planning learning and learner progress and satisfaction. Learning providers are very familiar with these frameworks and you will be able to work together to develop appropriate means of gathering evidence that fit with both learners' needs and MLA requirements, for instance using the Planning and Recording Learners' Achievements in Literacy, Language and Numeracy (PLRA) materials or Recognising and Recording Progress and Achievement in Non-accredited Learning (RARPA) frameworks.

Chapter eleven

Sustaining the work

You have achieved something good and you want to carry it on. It is important to start thinking about sustainability from the outset. Key elements for achieving this are:

- organisational commitment to the work;

- forging lasting partnerships;

- creating resources; and

- funding.

As you will see below, a key requirement for successfully getting access to funds is showing what you can offer in terms of knowledge, experience, and strong relationships with your partners. Thus the various aspects of sustainability are closely linked.

Funding is a fast-moving area, and if you are trying to secure grants you have to be prepared to keep abreast of what new money is available. An exhaustive examination of the sources of funding for learning in the MLA is beyond the scope of this guide, but here are a few general suggestions, followed by some websites that you might find useful to get you going. You will also find the regional Museums, Libraries and Archives Councils to be invaluable sources of information and guidance in relation to funding.

Building upon what you have already achieved

Although funding is always hard to come by, and is usually awarded on a project-by-project basis, institutions covered by the MLA umbrella have two important strengths that it is important to capitalise on.

First, at least some staff in these organisations are likely to be employed from core funding and may work full time. This means that you will be in a good position to build up expertise and to develop strong relationships with partner organisations. Over time, your staff and partners will gain a valuable stock of knowledge, for example through working on specific projects or through staff training in literacy, language and numeracy (see chapters seven and eight). This is an important resource, and the ability to demonstrate past experience, knowledgeable and aware staff, and an existing partnership that provides access to, for example, specialist literacy, language and numeracy tutors, will all improve your chances of gaining access to further funding.

Secondly, you may well be capitalising on one of the principal assets *already owned* by your institution: 'permanent collections'. These might be objects in a museum, or documents and images in an archive or library, which can be used as teaching resources. They may simply need packaging in a way that relates to literacy, language and numeracy to give a strong foundation for a funding proposal. Teaching resources tied to your permanent collections, and perhaps put in an accessible place such as on your institution's website, also enable your project to continue to have an impact after the funding has finished. They may allow you to continue developing strong links with potential partnership organisations, for instance colleges interested in bringing groups of students to your institution, and will certainly provide evidence of successful outcomes that will help with future funding applications.

Your partners might have access to funding for literacy, language and numeracy work or you might apply to make joint applications to strengthen the bid. Always make funding considerations and availability clear to partners right from the start, and never promise more than you are sure you can deliver.

Don't underestimate the time needed to work up a sound funding proposal. You need to consult with the communities you want to work with as well as your partners.

What money is available?

General websites

In addition to any established budget that your institution already has, your work with learners opens up the possibility of accessing other sources of money. The best way of exploring this is via the good 'portal' websites, which gather together information about a range of funding and present it in a clear, accessible and bite-sized way. These sites will enable you to get an impression of what is available at a glance.

- The *Read Write Plus* section of the Department for Education and Skills (DfES) website gives a fund-by-fund summary of what is available, and what it will support, as well as web links to individual websites for each

fund, initiative, or administering organisation. See:
www.dfes.gov.uk/readwriteplus/Planning_and_Funding

- The Grants On Line site provides full directories arranged by funder type (though access to these directories requires registration). See: www.grantsonline.org.uk

- The NIACE website includes a regularly updated summary of the major funders, and is probably the most instantly accessible. See: www.niace.org.uk/information/Guides/ExternalFunds/

- There is a good general guide to how to get funding on the GEM (Group for Education in Museums) website. See: www.gem.org.uk

Remember, if you are working with a partner they may well have a lot more experience applying for money than you do, and their expertise in fundraising might be something that you want them to bring to the partnership. You should also call on the expertise of your regional MLA.

Local Learning and Skills Councils

The Learning and Skills Council (LSC) is responsible for planning and funding all education and training apart from higher education for over 16 year olds in England. The LSC distributes funds through core and discretionary funding streams, and one of its priorities is adult literacy, language and numeracy.

Core funding is only awarded to approved providers who can satisfy the LSC's stringent targets, quality and information requirements. Partners such as adult education providers and colleges probably draw down core funding that could be used for joint provision.

LSC discretionary funds are for short-term project and development work and you might be eligible to apply for these funds. However, demand always exceeds the amount available so you will need an interesting and creative proposal that demonstrates how you will assist the LSC to meet their targets. But do avoid falling into the trap of tailoring funding projects to meet the needs of the funders rather than the learners.

It is also worth getting actively involved with your Local Learning Partnership or Local Strategic Partnership. Many Learning Partnerships have *Skills for Life* sub-groups, which might be able to access funding for targeted partnership bids. These groups might also be a source of funding for specialist professional development for staff.

Chapter twelve

Spreading the word

Working out what you achieved, and then spreading the word about it, is an important part of working with learners. Dissemination of your literacy, language and numeracy work:

▦ enables other people working in MLA organisations and learning providers to build on what you have done;

▦ can help you secure further funding; and

▦ can influence managers, policy makers and planners.

If you don't disseminate, your project will have an impact only upon the small group of people that it touches directly. Tell more people about your work, and the impact will be greatly magnified. There are many ways of publicising what you have done.

Working out what was valuable

Use the evidence you gathered to evaluate your work and consider how you can use it to demonstrate the value of your work to others. Be sure to include your partners' and learners' perspectives. Produce evidence that demonstrates the impact of your work and celebrates the benefits you each gained from working together.

Different approaches suit different purposes. Consider the audience and the impression you want to make when deciding how to gather and present evidence.

Websites

If your organisation has a website, make sure that the project gets a mention. Writing a case study (see p. 71) will provide you with a good piece of 'stand-alone' text and some illustrations which will make an ideal web page.

Events

Celebration events and conferences can bring people together from a range of backgrounds to learn from your experiences.

Talking to other professionals

Communicating with other professionals is an important strand in strengthening learning in museums, libraries and archives, and sharing good practice is a fundamental part of this. A good first port of call, if you have something to share, is your regional Museum, Library and Archive Council information about MLAs' regional structure, and contact details are available on the MLA's website, at: www.mla.gov.uk/action/regional/engreg.asp. The MLA are interested in gathering examples of literacy, language and numeracy projects, and may be able to point you in the direction of colleagues who will be interested in your work. The MLA may also be interested in a case study of your project, and you should talk to your local MLA office if you would be prepared to offer one.

Learning providers

It is also important to reach out to learning providers to inspire them to work with you. They should also be able to help you to get in touch with new learners, and may well be able to contribute specialist knowledge on literacy, language and numeracy for future work. Creating information aimed at them (perhaps outlining the possible learning potential of your collections, and the kind of work that you have done in the past) and making resources that they can use (such as the outcomes of previous projects) is a good way of engaging with providers. You might also be able to run workshops and training events that would enable you to make direct contact with tutors, or perhaps organise learning visits/taster sessions to demonstrate to tutors the value for students of your collections.

The local community

Although talking to other professionals is important, they are not the only audience you might want to approach. Below are a few other ideas:

- The local media are always happy to find a news story, and the success of a project run through your institution will almost always generate interest. Why not contact your local newspaper and radio or television station?

- Create a travelling exhibition of your work, or a video, that you can use to promote what you offer in local venues such as libraries, community centres, nurseries and schools.

- Organise a learners' celebration event, to focus upon the achievements of learners that you have worked with.

- Produce information in an accessible form – an attractive leaflet or flyer that can be easily distributed is a good way of disseminating what you have to offer.

- Use your community contacts and champions to spread the word.

- Make sure that you tell people with influence or funding to support your work such as the Learning and Skills Council, local councillors, and learning partnerships.

Writing a case study

Writing a case study about your project will help to clarify your thoughts about it, its successes, its failures, and whether or not it ultimately met its aims. It will give you a summary that you can use if other organisations or colleagues ask you about the project, and something that you can use to help you approach prospective partners in setting up future work. A case study can also make a good page on your website. Contact your regional MLA for a template for collecting case study material. There are several key points to remember when writing a case study. It should contain four principal elements:

- Background

- The aims of the project

- How it proceeded

- The outcomes

These four elements will allow you to draw out what it was about your project that was successful. 'Background' should give a brief indication of who you are, and the circumstances surrounding the decision to run the project. Did you identify a particular need in the community, and if so, how? Did you apply for funding, and if so, from whom? The 'Aims' element should give people ideas about what they might be able to aim for themselves. 'How it proceeded' should cover things like actual actions that you took to get the project up and running, which partners you worked with, and how effective that was, problems that you faced and overcame. In 'Outcomes', think broad. You touched the lives of a certain number of project members, but what happened to them afterwards? Did they go on to study, or to volunteer? Have they encouraged more people to visit your institution since? Perhaps the project is still running, but with less input from you now the members have taken over.

You should also try to collect appropriate images to illustrate your case study; photographs of the result of the project, or project members at work are particularly useful.

REMEMBER: Collect all evidence of dissemination that you can. Copies of case studies, internal reports, press cuttings, articles, or interviews with local media can all help you to get funding in the future!

Finally

In this publication we have aimed to demonstrate how adult learners, staff and volunteers can be inspired by the buildings, collections and treasures of museums, libraries and archives to develop high-quality, imaginative and effective approaches to literacy, language and numeracy development. We hope that you enjoy the challenge.

Further reading and surfing

There is a lot of literature on the subject of learning opportunities offered in MLA institutions, but here are a few starting points that may be of help.

The MLA website has a great many useful documents and is well worth a visit at **www.mla.gov.uk**. The section on learning and access is also particularly useful. Regional MLA websites can also be found at the following addresses:

East of England:	www.eemlac.org.uk
East Midlands:	www.emmlac.org.uk
London:	www.almlondon.org.uk
North East:	www.memlac.co.uk
North West:	www.nwmlac.org.uk
Northern Ireland:	www.nimc.co.uk
Scotland:	www.scottishmuseums.org.uk
South East:	www.semlac.org.uk
South West:	www.swmlac.org.uk
Yorkshire:	www.ymlac.org.uk

Inspiring Learning for All at **www.inspiringlearningforall.gov.uk** gives a comprehensive guide to delivering learning opportunities in MLA domain institutions.

You might also like to check out the GEM website at **www.gem.org.uk**, which, although focused on museums, contains much that will also be of interest to libraries and archives.

You might also like to look at the Department of Culture, Media and Sport website at **www.culture.gov.uk** which will give you an idea of government initiatives in the MLA domains. The Department for Education and Skills has published a number of free publications on different aspects of *Skills for Life* assessment, teaching and learning, details of which can be found on their 'Read Write Plus' website at **www.dfes.gov.uk/readwriteplus**

If you need practical assistance in the management of projects, or in organising outreach work, there are titles in the NIACE *Lifelines in Adult Learning* series that might help:

Eldred, J. (2005) *Developing Embedded Literacy, Language and Numeracy: Supporting Achievement,* Lifeline 21. NIACE.

Fincham, G. (2003) *Museums and Community Learning,* Lifeline 12. NIACE.

Lindsay, A. and Gawn, J. (2005) *Developing Literacy: Supporting Achievement,* Lifeline 18. NIACE.

McGivney, V. (2002) *Spreading the Word: Reaching Out to New Learners*, Lifeline 2. NIACE.

Newmarch, B. (2005) *Developing Numeracy: Supporting Achievement,* Lifeline 19. NIACE.

Windsor, V. and Healey, C. (2005) *Developing ESOL: Supporting Achievement,* Lifeline 20. NIACE.

See also:

Department for Education and Skills (2005) *Planning Learning and Recording Progress and Achievement: A Guide for Practitioners.* Department for Education and Skills.

Greenwood, M. and Wilson, P. (2004) *RARPA: Recognising and Recording Progress and Achievement in Non-accredited Learning. Evaluation Report on the RARPA Pilot Projects April 2003–March 2004.* NIACE and LSDA.

Glossary

Terms specific to this book

Core staff

Used in this text to refer to employed members of staff at museums, libraries and archives that are not dependant upon project funding.

Learning providers

Anyone (for example, FE colleges, ACL services, or private training firms) who provides learning opportunities.

Personal development

The growth of people as individuals, often resulting in greater self-confidence. Personal development may be encouraged by learning – and frequently informal experiences and non-accredited courses which are undertaken for pleasure. Can be an outcome of almost any learning; in addition, some learning sets out with personal development aims.

Social exclusion

This occurs when individuals, communities and/or neighbourhoods have become disengaged from wider society. Areas that suffer from social exclusion will often have access and involvement in low levels of services, and high crime rates. Those suffering from social exclusion will often have very low self-esteem, feeling that facilities open to all (such as museums and libraries) are not for them.

Useful terminology common to literacy, language (ESOL) and numeracy

Accreditation

Formal ways of recognising achievement or giving credit for learning.

Assessment tools

Ways of discovering individuals' strengths and weaknesses in a particular subject.

Basic skills

This term is often used to describe this area of work but many people find this a patronising or demeaning term. We have chosen to use the term literacy, language and numeracy in this publication as it describes the subject areas more accurately.

Common Inspection Framework for post-16 education and training

The standards by which the quality of teaching and learning in post-16 education is evaluated.

Deficit model

A model based on assumptions about what learners cannot do, rather than what they can do.

Diagnostic assessment

A more in-depth assessment that identifies not only strengths but also what a learner needs to work on, and which serves as the basis for drawing up a learning plan.

Differentiation

Providing a range of teaching approaches and learning materials that cater for different abilities and learning styles.

Discrete provision

Subject-specific provision, separate from other courses.

Dyslexia

Having difficulties that may affect the learning of reading, writing, spelling and/or numeracy.

Embedded provision

Where literacy, language or numeracy is linked to specific themes or contexts, often integrated with a vocational programme, an interest or workplace.

Formative assessment

Ongoing assessment to recognise progress and inform the next stage of teaching.

Ground rules

Mutually agreed code of behaviour for a group.

ICT/ILT

Information and communication technology/information and learning technology – the use of computers and other technology such as digital cameras, videos, interactive whiteboards, multimedia, and so on.

ILP

Individual learning plan.

Initial assessment

An assessment that gives a general picture of a learner's level to support referral to appropriate provision and provide starting points for learning.

Learning aim

Description of the purpose of a learning activity.

Learning objective

A statement describing a specific outcome intended as a result of learning, for example 'learners will be able to calculate percentages.'

Learning styles

Different ways of learning and accessing information which suit different people's strengths, which may be described as visual, auditory, or kinaesthetic.

Literacy, language and numeracy screening

A snapshot assessment to identify whether someone might want to develop their literacy, language and numeracy skills.

Progression routes

Where to go next, either in terms of future study or employment.

Reflective thinking

Assessing what you know, what you need to know, and how to bridge the gap.

Scheme of work

Outline of work to be covered on a course, showing intended sequence and organisation.

Skills for Life strategy

The government's national strategy for improving literacy, language and numeracy skills.

Spiky profile

Having a mixture of strengths and weaknesses, being good at some things and wanting to develop others.